bright news of gladiolas

July Westhale

Harbor Editions
Small Harbor Publishing

bright news of gladiolas
Copyright © 2021 JULY WESTHALE
All rights reserved.

Cover art by Alessandra Baragiotta
Cover design by Taylor Blevins
Book layout by Allison Blevins

BRIGHT NEWS OF GLADIOLAS
JULY WESTHALE
ISBN 978-1-7359090-1-1
Harbor Editions,
an imprint of Small Harbor Publishing

for Martin

CONTENTS

aerial view / 11

76 station, with the broken pump / 12

moon moon / 13

not all men / 14

when we reached the moon's moon, we were surprised it had two capital cities, like Bolivia / 15

bright news of gladiolas / 16

for the gift horse, whom I always shoot in the mouth / 17

from the mouth of the gift horse / 18

mindfulness practice / 19

____ truths and a lie, or, artichokes / 20

aubade for translation / 21

patron saint of drank-too-much / 22

awake in her / 23

aubade for the tree that will one day crush my house / 27

nobody move, there's blood on the floor and I can't find my heart / 28

roses are red because their ears are burning / 3

dark news like white warblers / 31

sweet & saline & rotten / 32

nocturne for the man who threw a brick through my front window
    last July / 34

try to praise / 35

bird's eye / 36

bright news of gladiolas

Nothing happened in the city today
unless you count the youth on a horse pushing
eleven cows across an intersection from
the field of rubble and plastic bags
to somewhere else.

"Nothing Happening" by Linda Gregg

aerial view

The cat who reigns from atop a prickly pear   the cat
who drinks deeply from the storm drain   the cat
who eats the birds in poems   with a side of petals
the cat   who chirps like a bird
the cat who leapt first, thought after   who mirrors the cat
that thought too long, missed the boat   which left on time, for once
after a diatribe on naps and napping   because of business
a curled-up vantage point, a wrap-around   porch and brittlebrush
the color of a 25-cent ochre gumball   perhaps we have it wrong
there are plenty of cats who make it   in a world lush, half-asleep—

76 station, with the broken pump
for Hayden Caruth

I just took my old hope out of the shop,
with her singular, dented-end situation,
and I was open, so to speak, for a crash test.

Loving along. The sky: an open body,
the road: a hot bed. Myself, alone
at a bar, hair high. Hope low. Just a little

air in the tires, that's all. Prepared
for the ruts, the tectonic malaise of boulevards.
Too close to home, kiddo, too close.

Might as well pawn this old gal now,
keep the breeze easy, as they say, the space
sheltered and calm. The body out of bounds.

My self wiggles like a scared rabbit.
But the day is a bright one, the clouds
are perfect memes of themselves, and everywhere

headlight-eyed pedestrians circumnavigate
the potholes, like willing clergy
of the world and its marvelous catastrophes,

in spite of the blow-outs, the bad road food,
bathrooms with windows that age faces,
the filling and emptying and filling again.

That's what gas stations are for. That,
and the lucky yellow numbers, spit out
and handed off by someone who couldn't care less.

It's still too goddamn close to home. I keep on.
A man on 27th and West holds a sign: *Anything?*
I wave and drive. Then I burst into tears.

moon moon

Now there's snow on the ocean, which is meant to confuse us
and does, though not because we are unprepared for it
but rather because the sight of it reminds us
of the static-hearted parts of our bodies as they prostrate
themselves in years-over-yonder: exploratory attempts
to find warmth—not unlike a surefooted expedition—,
in the disappearance of everything ripe (that is now covered
with snow's annihilating speeches), in the blank stares
of our children as they amputate themselves
from us, in the cloudscape of cum forgotten to be enjoyed,
on the snow of a down comforter at which we'd first begun
(circle back to exhibit A), in the cold expanse following
the question *am I like winter to you*, in the unspooling
that happens when we, I, I mean I play a memory
over again for the too-many-ith time, in the television's
convex and prudish eye, in the snowy sound of over-use,
in the way empty feels like brain-freeze, in the brilliant
and nearly-neon white of the sign which mourns *vacancy*
even if everyone around us says *off-season*, says they love

the snow, the way it makes well-conquered land possible again.

not all men

He isn't sexist, you say,   *The*
just an old letch. He loves   *call*
women. It won't stop   *is*
raining. There are awful blossoms   *coming*
spread-eagle on the road.   *from*
White bloom panties so prolific   *inside*
you'd have looked at it and thought: *the*
now there is a man who loves women. *house.*

when we reached the moon's moon, we were surprised it had two capital cities, like Bolivia

It was like stepping into a basin of lights, a bowl of half-dimmed stars, to the urban-dwellers among us. For the bucolicly-inclined, it
    was *too much*. But that was the thing

we enjoyed about it. Enjoy. Present-tense. Still enjoyable in the glass elevator of one's memory, even if there is a child at the helm,
    pushing all the buttons. You cannot

go up and down at the same time, but you can be surrounded by something that is so potently unique that it has its own year,
    takes its own time reaching your eyes. By that

I mean light. I mean a country with two capital cities. I mean the way you hold grapefruit—it knocks me out. However, it didn't hurt.
    Not only because we were in a foreign country.

But because I'm sorta invincible. Knocking or other-country. The other-country of a banging heart, or some place in my insides
    that feels knock-kneed.

The hollow bereavement of a city in blackout, say, or the turned-inside-out shake of standing after falling. Something continued to fall,
    straight to the earth, which is all light

molten and crushed-up, as though the inverse of La Paz is a mortar and pestle. Electricity an afterthought. Who am I kidding.
    We all feel this way.

bright news of gladiolas

Because it was not so yesterday
it bears saying: under the over-
pass, the blooms
of those returning to neoprene thickets,
blankets woven like flax fields
                        a city, a linocut

of the before times, when people could people.
The stanza breaks between metropolises,
wild. Purple-gray. Like the underside
                        of a redwood sorrel.

Proximity always matters,
but we don't remember. A man cuts the line
at the express lane, and I am quick
                        to anger. To forget

this is the reason one lives
in a city: high population purposefulness.

In the spaces between:
                the bus blurring buildings to   dense cliffs
                piles of coffee cups   like sheep
                bright news of   gladiolas
                orphaned tires singing *take*   *me home*

for the gift horse, whom I always shoot in the mouth

I never say never
always say *molars* say *flat tongue* say *measure*
note *heavy* note *hard-won*
note the vantage point of the desert at sun-up,
anatomical, metaphorical
say *velvet lips* say *restless*
say *point* say *boom*

from the mouth of the gift horse

[I *swear* I was once a colt, eyes to the mirrored
sky, fields of me with ropish legs, coming in
to the feed, the joyful feed, running like bulls
at a festival. The only hands on my flank,
tall grasses that played paramour, played lead,
no weight on my back but the world, which bowed
my body, both the arch of my spine and the curtain
call. Then the call came, which I heard because I am
god. The call and the trucks, the death mask so flies
could not eat my eyes, my brothers gone, no chance
to wave *farewell, farewell* and I *swear* the sky heaved
a pent-up sob, but that could just be Montana.
The rumble took me, I sweat and sweat in my clothes,
which smelled of other mustangs, other gifts,
and when we at last chanced upon California, a man
took my hood, and the poet opened my mouth
and shot me gone.]

mindfulness practice

and what if there are no books on the moon, are the books' feelings hurt? I am asking again if we can smell the moon, and does it smell like the library of Babel? And what does truth look like at the hands of gravity, and if all our systems are subject to the principles of floatation, then what does that say about presence? What does that say about us? The us-ness of us?

____ truths and a lie, or, artichokes

I chopped head after head, canceled
the gods for the day/ever. They blew
up my phone, which was in the drawer,
next to the knife. When at last I could stand
it no longer, I plunged my head
into white-capped dishwater. The rings
chopped and chopped. I choked. I never choke.

aubade for translation

here comes the mo(u)rning:
                      small suns in haloes (astigmatism)
                      space rendered through a fine sieve
                          of patient tongues
                      blue made universal

the pages are wet:
                      you
                      me
                      the poet's intention   does it matter

your love in her
                      stiff dress
                      cerecloth
                      habit   this is love   does it matter

patron saint of drank-too-much

Over here, solvent skyline. A virgin
in white, on a hill. Simple.

How cities seed. Every South American
epicenter, but usually a man,

a cross. An extended-release tab of guilt.
My neighbor, in the elevator: *how boring*

the martyred man. And, for that matter,
the elevator. I will remember this

for the rest of my life: ascent, descent,
the opening and closing of levels: yawn.

Share with me your yellowed paper book,
the gasp of a panorama, a just-peeled orange.

A solid replacement for falling in
over my head. This happens each time

like big wash-strokes of paint, adding
dimension to a landscape already too large

to bear, especially as my youth melts
from my body, and the filthiest and most

secret places in the city melt to meet the world,
I pay and I pay and I pay for trespasses of men

from my two countries and their bickering—still
I come back: Santiago eaten down to the root—

blame transubstantiation, or the women
who taught us all to dance first and talk later,

but never blame the poem. Not the first time,
nor after the poet dies. Decomposes.

Beware nostalgia, patron saint of drank-too-much.
It will make a Catholic of you. And you. And you.

Neruda loved a woman with a snake bouffant
mere blocks from my unfurnished studio

where the heat was killed nearly immediately
and stayed buried through every Andean winter.

Lucia Berlin described a Santiago as crisp
and pre-revolution as perfect toast, but I had

nothing to my name but a lover who wouldn't
fuck me, the virgin outside my window

an aubade and nocturne both. White white white.
One neighborhood over, they broke the fingers

of Victor Jarra, *the Woody Guthrie of Chile* because God
forbid he be the Victor Jarra of anything.

Up, then down. Open. Close. Boring.

Many things could not be true
but there you have it: in writing.

awake in her

A kind of purring, outside the sill
in a bright morning, so bright
it's as though something in the sky tore apart.

Still, the mourning doves. Always erroneous
birds of all-over, nowhere specific.
As a child, I believed my grandmother
placed them in mesquite, bougainvillea,
acacia, for me. Outside my guest sill,

in the white lie, the bright morning of childhood.
Somebody loved me enough to plant
birds that rumpled the air into murmurs,
a constant *there, there*. She is gone,
and they are otherwise known

as rain doves. This morning, awake in her
old neighborhood, the birds in their proper
places. A super bloom year, from so much
rain—the saguaros alight in grief flowers
so large they erase themselves.

aubade for the tree that will one day crush my house

Let it be said that night left you
unclothed and we deserve each other.

Each leaf serrates the sky's clouded loaves
and loves a gnarled root system that strangles

the sugar peas. Dragon lady with the Frida
body, the thick thighs and trunk and plentiful heads.

All night you hold a boombox to my window
and play anything but Etta James. Let it be

said that first there was light, then slightly more.
So in the dawn's rendering you are pastel

and confused. Secretly savoring the soil
of my basement's dampest parts, working those corked

fists into the boxes that bear names of other love
I played house with. You bleed as you rummage, hot and serious.

        Of course, we're dispossessed.
            What on Earth
            could keep us here?

nobody move, there's blood on the floor and I can't find my heart[1]

I like flowers   so what if I like   flowers
they aren't here to like me back   my back to everything
you mess   *I resent*
a cool calm voice   a reflective surface
so much of it
I am breathing in
why   I am breathing out
this is not what I cosigned   why   gosh it's *everywhere*

Stop.

Can you put one foot in front of the other
zip yourself inside the dirt devil, tasks and bills,
piece of shit lovers *all* made equal: a sonic
palpation of mere speed and your ear.
That's it. Sometimes staying calm
means getting inside and imagining a Doppler effect—
everything as detritus
                        which it is

No one is actually a piece of shit, just shit.
Just actual, literal shit. Which has no place
in a poem about meditation. Throw it
to the dirt devil, it too will whizz past your nose

                        but it won't smell   this is visualization

Use those same feet.
One, then the other.
The devil keeps on keeping on. He doesn't
even have a rearview mirror to throw a glare back.

---

[1] Thundercat

There it is, at last:

the clean cotton field. Crisp, pulled taut. Utterly stainless.

roses are red because their ears are burning[2]

forgiveness is a small
price to pay
for using a metaphor
when the nearest exit
may be in the world left behind.

Remember urbanity? Recitations
of roses, embarrassed or not,
poetry's broken spine
staring at the cracks in the sidewalk
as we walked, surely breaking
our mothers' backs,
if we had mothers.

Retrospect is a fable,
I mean fabulous, origin story
through another's verse,
and thank heavens for it—
for without, we'd be lost,
or worse, we'd misunderstand.

---

[2] Laura Jensen

dark news like white warblers

Lazy white warblers in the jade tree,
dozens on Telegraph, passing gossip,
passing time, watching me pass them
with my earphones as if I'm connected
to the world inside, wounded

with bliss. Or a bouquet of men in stains
under the overpass, laughing. Passed
over, overlooked. Dandelions in haloes,
mustard in sharpness. Creative in cracks

of purple pavement. The real Spring brings
clean blooms to the cherry trees, corsage
of debris at the base, a blurt of spray paint
cross-pollinating: *Show Ur Tits.*

Good thing roses are never scarce
in California. As if something so openly bloody

could cease cyclically, like that. And if it does—
as if the fresh wool of the world
wouldn't come calling, come to wipe tidy
the marvelous simplicity of us all.

      Talking to you is like being alone.
      No matter how many times I switch
      on the lights, the cockroaches run,
      in surprise, for their lives.

sweet & saline & rotten

For years I've driven by the Beach Chalet,
        said *have you said hello to the Diego?*

—

If you want to see some of the last remaining American bison, you would do well to go ten miles, not to the vast plains of Willa Cather or the poems of Joy Harjo, but to the outside lands. They are every bit as craggy as the city of San Francisco: shaggy noses, their prehistoric faces, always perfectly lit with soft light and fog, a small cut of blocky houses visible through the eucalyptus groves, reminding us we're still in a city, these animals are still extinct. Which makes me remember the barbed wire, how I can only see their grand humped hefts if I close one eye and squint with the other through the coated fencing I want, vehemently, to bite into. I want to touch them. I know why I can't. I think, erroneously, that I'm the exception to the rule that humanity is terrible. *Is the cow sleeping or throwing up?* (this was a child but could have been anyone).

They're just happy.

—

Thick on extinction/hubris, we go to see the Diego.

which smells sweet and saline and rotten,
like the ocean, the ocean across the street,
        the noise indistinguishable from tourists
slow-cruising in their rented Miatas,
        determined to have a Californian experience,
knowing nothing of the city in "summer."

—

For years I've passed by with friends or visitors, pointed to the grand Beaux Arts façade and said, *there's a Diego Rivera inside, aren't we lucky?*

—

Now here we are. The Diego, colors on mute,
all fresco, ocean town in June.

        San Francisco Life, it says, writ large. By Lucien Labaudt.

nocturne for the man who threw a brick through my front
    window last July

all night I quietly searched for the idea of *stars* to find a translation
the poet from Patagonia might have wanted:
            jacks, or losing at jacks
            the palpable difference in skies between hemispheres
            headlights on rural roads when the deepest night turns
            its back from loving you
            a hangover behind the eyes
            the world before the internet
            cream clots before they are swallowed by coffee
and then the thin glass, like uterine lining, or a phone call
exploding into millions of them, beaming and resplendent and
prismatic—

try to praise

the year of red courtesans, rows
                of sunflowers, their god-given
                mourning faces.

The bounce and force with which a river
pushes back. Praise turgid tides
as they crescendo, hold back, are too emotive,
then not enough.
                How the world bruises too easily!
                How could it not? Much effort

lives secreted in the world, attempts to bottle
itself. Volcanos can't stay quiet forever.

Those who know that best are the dead,
jail-broken bodies who've seen the bow and bend
of love in its tender iterations:

the precious circadian rhythms of birds leaving home/returning
the monarchs who've landed in eucalyptus townships
the ancient wisdom of winter and its dark inversion.

Try to praise the tender world its summits
and fault lines—the angelic face of summer solstice
and dank basement of snow alike. Do it in recitation,
not for those gone, but so that they can be gone
in good faith. That we might remember them
in the world's profile, in her likeness.

So we might say we lived
when you did not, in the most vulnerably obliterating
way we could—which is to say, in praise of you.

bird's eye

One could say the pond was waiting. One could say it was a pond at all. We're waiting, water brides, in wedges, with our feet going going going under us, which you'd not be able to tell from above water. As a careful observer, you'd see a congregation like any grouping of birds together the ways birds are often ominously together on large seawalls, jetties, the communion-wafer of telephone wires. *What on Earth could they be talking about?* It's a trick question. Our conversation is never of Earth. We're talking about your bald spots, your poorly-shingled rooftops. When in water, we're watching to see if you'll break all of the rules of sense and feed us squares of white bread or stale popcorn. We're watching to see the moment feeding time bonds you to your child, what kind of stand-in parenting our presence, our gobbling at the silvery surface can give to you. Since the first canonized myth, we are also warily watching, waiting for godlike men to trespass. We beak our feathers to meringue tufts. We emerge from the pond, shake and shake, stretch our wings, pick the dirt and bugs out, rearrange. The barnacle geese look on. Jealously. There are no myths about barnacle geese. No one comes to feed them to save their marriage. And therein lies the difference: *we live to serve.*

ACKNOWLEDGMENTS

This book would not have been possible without the small village that always assists any manuscript being produced. A few on the short list include: Allison Blevins and the fine team at Harbor Editions, AC Panella, Joey Gould, Carl Phillips, Pam Houston, and Dana Belott. Funding and community support came from the Bay Area Writing Project, the Author's Guild, and the Tom and Evelyn Newberry fellowship through Writing By Writers.

Grateful acknowledgement is made to the editors at *DIAGRAM* and *Open Arts Forum*, in which versions of these poems first appeared.

July Westhale is an essayist, translator, and the award-winning author of *Trailer Trash* and *Via Negativa*, which Publishers Weekly called "stunning" in a starred review. Her most recent work can be found in *McSweeney's*, *The National Poetry Review*, *Prairie Schooner*, *CALYX*, *Hayden's Ferry Review*, and *The Huffington Post*, among others. She also has an inventively-named collection of salty chapbooks. When she's not teaching, she works as a co-founding editor of *PULP Magazine*. www.julywesthale.com

www.ingramcontent.com/pod-product-compliance
Lightning Source LLC
Chambersburg PA
CBHW051705040426
42446CB00009B/1322